The Romance of

Oxford

Guide and Souvenir

Published by
Chris Andrews Photographic Art
16 Hill View Road, Oxford, OX2 0BZ

The Romance of Oxford, Romantic Oxford and *The Romance of*
have trade mark application No's
1212352, 1212353 and 1231920 respectively.

ISBN 0 9509643 0 1

Front cover: Nuffield College, Oxford
The Spire at sunrise

Back cover: The Sheldonian Theatre,
Broad Street, Oxford

Typeset and printed by
S & S Press, Abingdon, Oxfordshire

MANY visitors come to Oxford expecting to find just a university . . . Matthew Arnold's 'sweet city with her dreaming spires'. Most will leave having discovered much more—the beauty and solitude of parks and meadows; an attractive and busy shopping centre; the serenity of the river, even a bewildering one-way traffic system! For modern Oxford is unique, a singular blend of the educational, industrial and commercial.

Few people, however, capture the tricks and the moods that early morning light—and the changing seasons—give to so many parts of the city.

This is the very special mark of photographic artist Chris Andrews.

He turns the seemingly ordinary into a scene which is clearly extraordinary, and his views of Oxford—both familiar and unfamiliar—are as diverse and fascinating as the city itself.

Oh ye spires of Oxford! domes and towers!
gardens and groves! your presence overpowers
the soberness of reason.
(William Wordsworth)

Oh Oxford, thou art lovely still,
For, ever round thy classic towers
Fond Nature with her utmost skill
   The richest gems upon thee showers·
Mid verdure bright on every hand
   Thy Colleges and Churches stand
(Henry W. Taunt)

And that sweet City with her dreaming spires,
   she needs not June for beauty's heightening
(Matthew Arnold)

A typical paradox is the picture of Nuffield College (front cover). Architecturally, the building is considered almost austere. But when viewed from the river at sunrise, the spire assumes a haunting and mysterious quality.

The college was founded in 1937 by Lord Nuffield, formerly William Morris, whose car-manufacturing empire gave rise to what is now the giant BL complex at Cowley. It was on his insistence that the college's design was kept unfussy and functional, though a notable contributor was John Piper who styled the windows, and whose work on the modern Coventry Cathedral is internationally acknowledged.

Nuffield certainly gave a new look to the immortal city skyline, pictured from South Park. Prominent among the city's spires are Magdalen College tower, Nuffield College tower, Lincoln College Library, The Wesley Memorial Church and The University Church of St. Mary the Virgin, and show how inextricably the Church and university are linked.

Towery city and branchy between towers;
Cuckoo-echoing, bell-swarmèd, lark-charmèd, rook-racked,
river-rounded . . .

(Gerard Manley Hopkins)

Oxford's history dates back as far as the early 10th century when it was chronicled as a place where people and oxen could safely cross the river — hence oxen-ford.

But those who believe that the modern town owes its existence to the university would be mistaken. Religious communities existed before the Norman Conquest, and university colleges were in fact preceded by monastic 'halls' — places where people who came to Oxford to study (particularly theology) could be accommodated.

Left: Oxford from South Park.

Once established, the university gradually acquired independence and strength, backed by the Crown. It gave rise to an uneasy relationship between Town and Gown, culminating in bloody riots in the 13th and 14th centuries. Things didn't settle down in fact until the Test Act of 1672, which required all students to adhere to the thirty-nine articles of the Church of England. But the sense of rivalry remained, and Town v Gown 'battles' on the sports field continue to this day.

With the university having developed within the confines of the city, there is no 'campus'—a fact which confuses many visitors to Oxford. Educational and commercial interests go hand in hand. Broad Street, in the heart of the city, reflects this co-habitation particularly well.

Within just 200 metres you will find Balliol and Trinity Colleges, the New Bodleian Library and the Sheldonian Theatre interspersed with bookshops, such as Blackwell's, Parker's, and The Paperback shop, sports outfitters and tailors.

Running parallel to the Broad is High Street, in which is situated one of the city's most prominent landmarks, St Mary's Church, pictured from Oriel Street. (See over-leaf)

This lovely 13th century building was the lecture hall of the mediaeval university. Today it is the official university church, and the start of each term is marked by a service there. St. Mary's imposing 180ft spire and delightful architecture are big tourist attractions, and it is notable to historians for the fact that John Wycliffe preached there—and was also the starting point for the unfortunate Protestant Martyrs' walk to the stake.

Above left: St. Giles.

Below left: Broad Street.

The University
Church,
St. Mary the Virgin
from Oriel Street.

The city rose in terraces
Of radiant buildings, backed with towers
And dusky folds of elm-tree bowers.
St Mary's Watchmen, mute and old,
Each rooted to a buttress bold,
From out their lofty niche looked down
Upon the calm monastic town,

(Frederick W. Faber)

Sheldonian Theatre, Broad Street.

The Sheldonian Theatre in Broad Street is one of the finest—and earliest—examples of the work of Sir Christopher Wren. Its name is slightly misleading, for although some concerts are held there, it is not strictly a theatre. It is mainly used by the university for degree ceremonies, particularly the granting of honorary titles at the annual Encaenia.

The Sheldonian has an impressive ceiling, painted by Robert Streeter, which is meant to look like the sky—thus suggesting an open air theatre.

A particular boon to tourists is that they can climb to the roof, from where they get an excellent panorama of the city.

Lovers of architecture, music and real ale are inevitably drawn to Holywell Street at the end of Broad Street. There are more examples of 17th and 18th century building here than in any other street in central Oxford, and to catch a glimpse of the styles and colours of the facades in early morning is to turn the clock back two or three hundred years.

Situated in the street is the Holywell Music Room, founded in the middle 18th century specifically for the giving of musical concerts. And 240 years later it is still fulfilling that purpose.

Many undergraduates, however, merely look upon the street as a thoroughfare between favourite watering holes . . . the Kings Arms and the Turf Tavern. The Turf enjoys one of the quaintest positions of any pub in the country—tucked among the leaning 16th and 17th century houses of Bath Place . . . a narrow cobbled court leading directly off Holywell Street, with another exit to New College Lane.

Continuing towards Radcliffe Square is the Bridge of Sighs, joining the two parts of Hertford College.

Noon strikes on England, noon on Oxford town
Proud and godly kings had built her long ago
With her towers and tombs and statues all arown'
With her fair and floral air and the love that lingers there
And the street where the great men go

(James Elroy Flecker)

Right: Holywell Street.

A university's greatest need is for a comprehensive collection of books, and in the Bodleian, Oxford has one of the most impressive libraries in the world. It was founded by an Elizabethan scholar, Sir Thomas Bodley, who set about restoring a collection which had been all but destroyed in the Reformation—Edward VI considering many of the works in the original library as being too 'Popish'.

The Bodleian is entitled to a copy of every book published in the country—one of only six libraries nationwide to be accorded this privilege. It now houses more than two million volumes.

Such is the vastness of the modern library, it occupies three sites linked by a system of tunnels to facilitate the easy passage of books.

One of these three is arguably Oxford's most famous landmark, the Radcliffe Camera in Radcliffe Square. The Camera was founded in the 18th century from money given by Dr John Radcliffe, physician to King William III and Queen Anne, and whose name was given to the city's two major hospitals. It is now one of the Bodleian's reading rooms.

The Bodleian does not follow the traditions of modern libraries, in that no book can be borrowed . . . only read on the premises. Even then, people who wish to read the books must be able to provide references, and promise not to kindle a fire in the buildings!

City of weathered cloister and worn court;
　　Grey city of strong towers and clustering spires;
Where art's fresh loveliness would first resort;
　　Where lingering art kindled her latest fires

Like to a queen in pride of place, she wears
　　The splendour of a crown in Radcliffe's dome.
Well, fare she well! As perfect beauty fares;
　　And those high places, that are beauty's home.
(Lionel Johnson)

Left: Radcliffe Square from Catte Street, showing St. Mary's Church and the Radcliffe Camera.

Brasenose Lane leads from Radcliffe Square to Turl Street. The glory of the lane, to anyone who has been frustrated by the city's unremitting traffic congestion, is that it is closed to motor vehicles—giving visitors at least a hint of the appearance of old Oxford.

Brasenose Lane, leading to Radcliffe Square.

Left: The Rooftops of Oxford, with the Radcliffe Camera, St Mary's Church and the twin towers of All Souls.

City of wildest sunsets,
which do pile
   Their dark-red castles
   on that woody brow!
Fair as thou art in summer's
moonlight smile,
   There are a hundred
   cities fair as thou,
But still with thee alone,
all seasons round,
Beauty and change in their
own right abound.

      (Frederick W. Faber)

Oxford at sunset.

Linking Broad Street and the High Street is the Turl—a narrow gateway which leads to some of Oxford's most interesting sights. The street itself, though small, contains three university colleges— Lincoln, Jesus and Exeter, all of which are worth a visit.

Jesus was founded by Queen Elizabeth I in 1571, and ranks among its notable students T.E. Lawrence (of Arabia). His portrait still hangs in the college hall, together with one of Charles I painted by Vandyck.

The founding of Lincoln College in 1427 was more than tinged with religious 'aggression'. It was the brainchild of Richard Flemyng, Bishop of Lincoln who wanted to counter the teachings of Wycliffe. The college Hall (1437) is the oldest in the university, though even that must give more than 100 years to the kitchen, which is recorded as early as 1300.

To the right of the Turl as you walk towards the High is Market Street leading to the covered market, wherein you can buy all manner of fresh meat, fish, vegetables and fruit or browse for a bargain among the stalls of furniture, jewellery and leather goods. The land on which it stands was set aside for the express purpose of getting the market off the streets, and it remains one of the city's most popular attractions.

> . . . Yet have I seen no place, by inland brook,
> Hill-top or plain, or trim arcaded bowers,
> That carries age so nobly in its look
> As Oxford with the sun upon her towers.
>
> (Frederick W. Faber)

Right: Turl Street, showing the spire of Lincoln College Library and Jesus College.

Christ Church is the university's largest college, and is known to the students simply as 'The House'—its full name being properly 'The House of Christ's Cathedral in Oxford'

There is much to admire in the buildings. Dominating the college quad, and the Oxford skyline, is Tom Tower—a bell tower begun by Cardinal Wolsey and finished by Sir Christopher Wren.

Though the Cathedral is the smallest of the older English Cathedrals, the college is the richest and largest in the university.

And bright rose the towers
    through the half-stripped bowers,
and the sun on the windows danced;
the churches looked white
in the morning light
    And the gilded crosses glanced.
(*From Christ Church Meadows* Frederick W. Faber)

Christ Church from the meadows.

Right:
The Cathedral from Tom Gate, Christ Church.

The original number of students at Christ Church in the 17th century was 101, and each evening since then at five past nine the bell is rung 101 times, to warn members that the gates of 'The House' are about to close.

The college, like Tom Tower, was originally founded by Wolsey who wanted to create the most magnificent college in the country. But he fell from favour only four years after work was begun in 1525, and the college was 're-founded' by Henry VIII in 1532.

The kitchen, however, has changed little since Wolsey's day and still contains the original, enormous fireplace. Equally impressive are the carved roof of the Hall, and the college's collection of paintings—including works by Thomas Gainsborough and Sir Joshua Reynolds. There is also a portrait by Millais of William Gladstone—one of the members of Christ Church to become Prime Minister.

Christ Church stretches from St. Aldates eastwards until it reaches the Oriel Square end of Merton Street. It is appropriate that Merton, the oldest university college, should be found in Oxford's last remaining cobbled street. Merton dates from 1264 and its library is one of the oldest in England. Historians will note that the Lollards were a force in the college in the 15th century, until their leader John Wycliffe was denounced and his works destroyed.

Oxford became the international centre for the study of astronomy and mathematics in the Middle Ages, because of the work of students at Merton College.

A feature of the ancient library is that many of the original books are still there, chained to the shelves. Books in mediaeval times were a precious commodity, and liable to be stolen.

Right: Oxford's only remaining cobbled street, Merton Street.

Merton College tower with Corpus Christi College on the right.

Next door to Merton College, on the corner of Oriel Square, stands Corpus Christi College, founded by Richard Fox, Bishop of Winchester and Keeper of the Privy Seal to both Henry VII and Henry VIII. He intended the college to be solely for students of theology although he was subsequently persuaded to broaden his views, and it then included the study of languages and classics. Among Corpus Christi's many eminent scholars was Thomas Arnold, the famous Headmaster of Rugby School.

One of the college's outstanding features of historical and architectural interest is a sundial in the front quadrangle which includes a perpetual calendar.

Magdalen College from the High.

Many visitors consider the most attractive college to be Magdalen, the first college encountered when entering Oxford by the original London road. Views of the college tower, from the river alongside, are some of the most familiar and popular.

The bell tower, with a peal of ten, was completed while Wolsey was junior bursar at the college. It is most famous for being the focal point of the city's May day celebrations. Each year, at dawn on May 1, the college choir sings anthems from the top of the tower to a large crowd of revellers below.

Another annual tradition is the preaching of a sermon on the feast day of St John the Baptist from an open-air, canopied pulpit in the college's old quadrangle. The college was built between 1467 and 1510 on a site formerly occupied by the Hospital of St John, parts of whose walls are still visible in the present building. There is also an archway, now bricked up, in the outside wall from which food was distributed to the poor in the 14th century.

Magdalen has a fine cloister as well as extensive gardens and grounds, including a deer park, which allows the visitor some unrivalled walks alongside the Cherwell.

Magdalen College from Merton Field.

Close by is the Botanic Garden, founded by the Earl of Danby in the 17th century for the propagation of medicinal herbs and plants. Time has seen the function of the Garden enlarge and expand, and it now includes a laboratory and famous botanic library.

> What city boasts herself the peer of thee,
> Dear Oxford, when the mist of morning clings
> Round Magdalen elms, or when the even flings
> Her rosy robe on river, hill and lea? . . .
>
> (James Williams)

One of the more singular features of Oxford is the existence of an enormous open grassland—Port Meadow—very near the heart of the city. The meadow has been owned by the Freemen of the City for more than a thousand years—thus precluding the possibility of individual ownership and therefore development.

So it remains relatively unspoilt as grazing land for cattle and horses, and a perfect retreat for weekend walkers. The Thames runs beside the meadow, and as well as the attraction of the solitude the place offers, there are excellent views of the city skyline from various points along its length.

One notable day in the year, when the meadow is anything but peaceful at its northern end, is the occasion in August when the Sheriff of Oxford's races are held there. Amateur riders compete in a series of races round the meadow on their own horses. The prizes are small, but the competition fierce and the betting heavy!

Oxford stands on both river and canal, and so there is no shortage of boating activities. One of the most picturesque sights is a university rowing week which takes place twice a year in February and May on the Thames below Folly Bridge. College eights row up from Iffley Lock while coaches shout their instructions from the adjacent tow path and crowds shout their encouragement from the banks. For the less ambitious water sportsman there is always the punt—a river craft traditional in both Oxford and Cambridge. Most visitors are familiar with the method—and hazards—of propelling the pole-driven craft, and usually have a go themselves.

Oxford's canal was opened in the 18th century and was used primarily to transport coal and other goods to and from the Midlands. The demise of the waterways for commercial transport merely gave rise to the development of a leisure industry and all manner of pleasure craft and narrow boats now use the canal.

Above right: Port Meadow.

Below right: Isis Lock on the Oxford canal.

Carfax and the High Street.

St. Giles.

Oxford

Main University Area

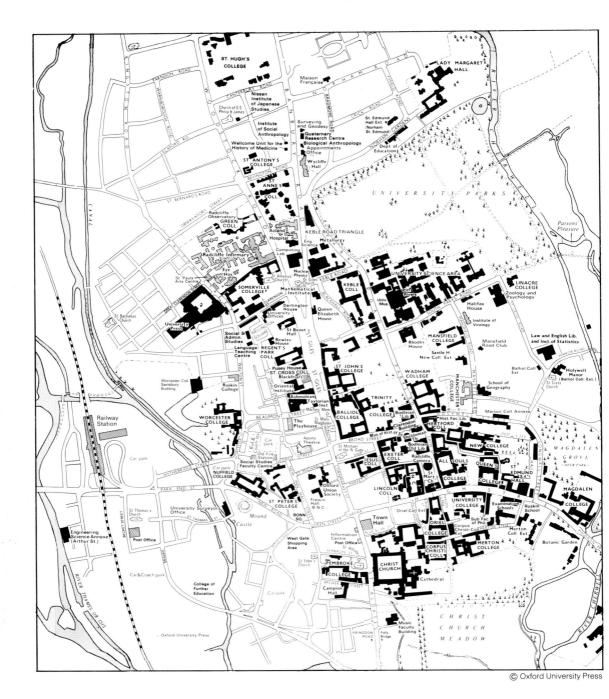